A gift for:

From:

Date:

Love That WORD

12 Simple WORDS to Inspire Your Christian Journey

SANDRA GLADDEN

Love that **WORD**

Copyright © 2019 by Sandra Gladden

Published by Sandra Gladden
www.lovethatWORD.org

All rights reserved. No portion of this publication may be reproduced, stored in a retrieval system or transmitted in any form by any means- electronic, mechanical, photocopying, recording, or any other- except brief quotations in printed reviews, without the prior permission of the publisher. The only exception is brief quotations in printed reviews.

Unless otherwise noted, Scripture taken from the New King James Version®. Copyright © 1982 by Thomas Nelson. Used by permission. All rights reserved.

WORDS OF CHRIST IN RED

The background Scripture on cover and interior pages are Scripture quotations taken from the New American Standard Bible® (NASB), Copyright © 1960, 1962, 1963, 1968, 1971, 1972, 1973,1975, 1977, 1995 by The Lockman Foundation. Used by permission. www.Lockman.org

Photos taken by Sandra Gladden on Holy Land Pilgrimage 2018

Book Cover and Interior Design by
Brian Dominey Design | www.briandominey.com

ISBN: 978-1-7338915-0-9

BOOK DEDICATION

To my heavenly Father, my sweet Jesus and my precious Holy Spirit: May I be about Your business and glorify You all the days of my life. I look forward to spending eternity in Heaven with You.

I love You,
Sandra

...rest, lest anyone fall through ...the same ªexample of ᵇdisobed...

12 For ªthe word of God is ᵇliving and active and sharper than any two-edged ᵈsword, and piercing as far as the division of ᵉsoul and ᵉspirit, of both joints and marrow, and ᶠable to judge the thoughts and intentions of ...heart. 13 And ªthere is no creatu... ...en from His sight, but all th... ...and laid bare to the ...

CONTENTS

Preface

12 Simple Words to Love and Live by...

WORD 1

BREATH 9

HOLY SPIRIT 17

HUMBLE 25

GRACE 33

GIFT 41

LIGHT 49

JOY 57

FAITH 65

HOPE 73

TRUST 81

LOVE 89

Closing Humble Prayer 97

PREFACE

In spring of 2017, God began challenging me with a question… "Who is your Master?"
After much soul searching, I discovered that I was truly serving man instead of God. Even though I love God, I love His Word and I call Him Lord of my life, I was allowing myself, my circumstances, my career and others to rule and reign most days of my life. During this same time frame, Meme, my precious 100-year-old Grandmother, was called home. We buried her and had her memorial service on Mother's Day; what an honor to reflect back on her life on such an appropriate holiday. The passing of a precious loved one also causes us to think on eternity and things of eternal value. For years, while reflecting on Scripture during my quiet times with God, I jotted down words in an acrostic format. After her passing, while reflecting on Meme's life, I wrote an acrostic to honor some life lessons that I had learned from her:

Mostly keep things SIMPLE
Every situation can be met with KINDNESS
Make JOY your motto
Everyone IS special and deserves a warm WELCOME

In transitioning my thought process to eternal values, I began to ask myself, *What really matters in life?* God created us to glorify Him. How do we do this best? Micah 6:8 tells us to walk humbly with God, to do the right thing and to love mercy. As a matter of fact, the entire Bible teaches and counsels us on how to do this journey of life and how to do it abundantly. God sent His only begotten Son to die for us so that we can have abundant life, not just in eternity, but also in the here and now. We get so bogged down in this world and forget to run to Him and His Word first, for the fruit of His Spirit that we need for each step of this journey…the Love, the Joy, the Peace, the Patience, the Kindness, the Goodness, the Faithfulness, the Gentleness and the Self-control.

So, in this quest to set my priorities in order and truly honor God as the Master of my life, I realized that the only infallible, inerrant Source to turn my focus to is My Savior and His Word. The humble example set by Jesus Christ can guide our way and free us to have a more abundant life. In addition to staying in my Bible, talking to my sweet Savior, hiding His Word in my heart and telling others about what He does for me as I go throughout each day, God has impressed upon my heart to write some of His Words of encouragement with the use of simple acronyms for His glory. Hopefully, *Love that **WORD***, will continue to deepen the desires of myself and readers to walk closely with God as we attempt to abundantly journey each day on this side of eternity. I pray that you will be blessed with a sense of His nearness and that you will enjoy these nuggets of truth from His Word as much as I enjoyed communing with my sweet Holy Spirit while writing them. To God be the glory!

Blessings to you and yours,

Sandra Gladden

...anyone fall throug...
...ame ªexample of ᵇdisobe...
For ªthe word of God is ᵇliving ...
active and sharper than any tw...
edged ᵈsword, and piercing as far as
the division of ᵉsoul and ᵉspirit, of
both joints and marrow, and ᶠable to
judge the thoughts and intentions o...
...heart. 13 And ªthere is no creatu...
...en from His sight, but all th...
... and laid bare to th...

WISDOM OF RIGHTEOUS DEITY

WORD

WISDOM OF RIGHTEOUS DEITY

In the beginning was the **WORD**, and the **WORD** was with God, and the **WORD** was God.

John 1:1

WISDOM OF RIGHTEOUS DEITY

Wisdom
Of
Righteous
Deity

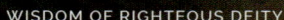

And the **WORD** became flesh and dwelt among us, and we beheld His glory, the glory as of the only begotten of the Father, full of grace and truth.

John 1:14

WISDOM OF RIGHTEOUS DEITY

For the **WORD** of God is living and powerful, and sharper than any two-edged sword, piercing even to the division of soul and spirit, and of joints and marrow, and is a discerner of the thoughts and intents of the heart.

Hebrews 4:12

WISDOM OF RIGHTEOUS DEITY

WORD

Humble Prayer

O Lord, thank you for Your righteous, living and holy WORD. Please open my mind and heart to understanding Your WORD so that I can follow You wholeheartedly each passing hour of my journey here on earth. May I always run to You and Your WORD first for advice and counsel, because You alone are sovereign and You know best.

In sweet Jesus' name I pray, Amen.

*By the **WORD**
of the Lord
the heavens were made,
And all the host
of them by the
BREATH of His mouth.*

Psalm 33:6

BOUNTIFUL RIGHTEOUS EMMANUEL ALWAYS TRULY HOVERS

BREATH

BOUNTIFUL RIGHTEOUS EMMANUEL ALWAYS TRULY HOVERS

*The Spirit of God has made me, And the **BREATH** of the Almighty gives me life.*

Job 33:4

BOUNTIFUL RIGHTEOUS EMMANUEL ALWAYS TRULY HOVERS

Bountiful
Righteous
Emmanuel
Always
Truly
Hovers

BOUNTIFUL RIGHTEOUS EMMANUEL ALWAYS TRULY HOVERS

*And the Lord God formed man of the dust of the ground, and **BREATHED** into his nostrils the **BREATH** of life; and man became a living being.*

Genesis 2:7

Thus says God the Lord, Who created the heavens and stretched them out, Who spread forth the earth and that which comes from it, Who gives **BREATH** to the people on it, And spirit to those who walk on it.

Isaiah 42:5

BOUNTIFUL RIGHTEOUS EMMANUEL ALWAYS TRULY HOVERS

BREATH

Humble Prayer

Dear God, I am nothing without You. You are Mighty Emmanuel. You formed me out of the dust of the earth. You BREATHED Your very BREATH into me. May I die to myself daily and let Your living waters flow through me so that You alone can be glorified. Thank You, Lord, for all that You are and all that You do.
In Jesus' name I pray, Amen.

HONORED ONE LOVINGLY YIELDED
SAVIOR'S PRESENCE INDWELLING & REIGNING IN TRUTH

And when He had said this, He **BREATHED** on them, and said to them, "Receive the **HOLY SPIRIT**."

John 20:22

HONORED ONE LOVINGLY YIELDED
SAVIOR'S PRESENCE INDWELLING & REIGNING IN TRUTH

HOLY SPIRIT

HONORED ONE LOVINGLY YIELDED
SAVIOR'S PRESENCE INDWELLING & REIGNING IN TRUTH

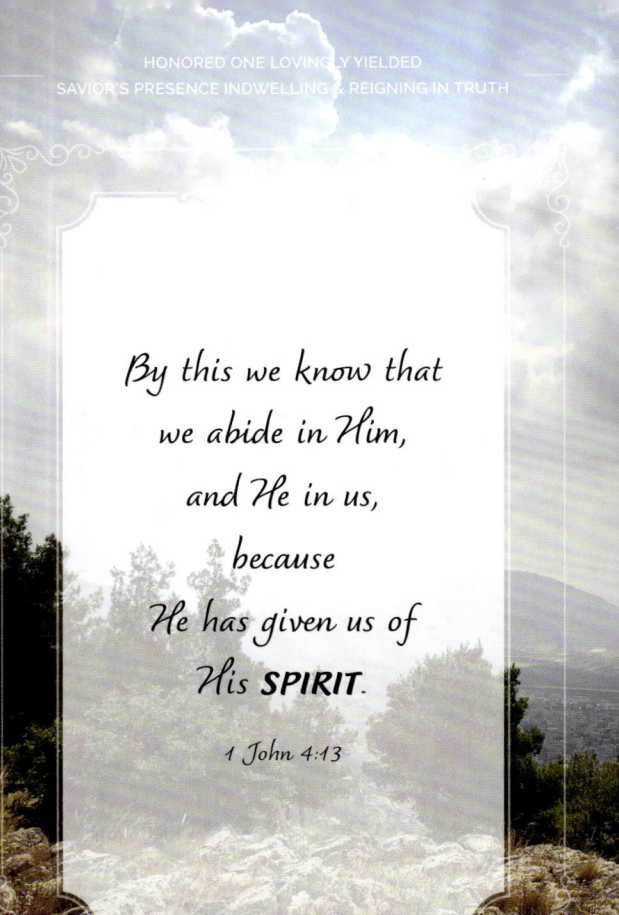

*By this we know that we abide in Him, and He in us, because He has given us of His **SPIRIT**.*

1 John 4:13

HONORED ONE LOVINGLY YIELDED
SAVIOR'S PRESENCE INDWELLING & REIGNING IN TRUTH

Honored
One
Lovingly
Yielded

Savior's
Presence
Indwelling &
Reigning
In
Truth

HONORED ONE LOVINGLY YIELDED
SAVIOR'S PRESENCE INDWELLING & REIGNING IN TRUTH

*In Him you also trusted, after you heard the **WORD** of truth, the gospel of your salvation; in whom also, having believed, you were sealed with the*

HOLY SPIRIT

of promise.

Ephesians 1:13

HONORED ONE LOVINGLY YIELDED
SAVIOR'S PRESENCE INDWELLING & REIGNING IN TRUTH

*"But the Helper, the **HOLY SPIRIT**, whom the Father will send in My name, He will teach you all things, and bring to your remembrance all things that I said to you."*

John 14:26

HONORED ONE LOVINGLY YIELDED
SAVIOR'S PRESENCE INDWELLING & REIGNING IN TRUTH

HOLY SPIRIT

Humble Prayer

O HOLY SPIRIT, may I learn to live each day acknowledging Your Presence living in me. May all that I say, think and do be well pleasing to You, Lord, my unlimited and resourceful Helper. May I humbly enjoy You and always make You feel welcome as You lead me daily. Thank You for choosing to make Your home in my life, sweet Jesus. I love you, Amen.

Blessed are the poor in spirit, for theirs is the Kingdom of heaven

A man's pride
will bring him low,
But the **HUMBLE** in
SPIRIT
will retain honor.

Proverbs 29:23

HOLY & USABLE for MASTER'S BOUNTIFUL LOVE EVERYDAY

HUMBLE

For thus says the High and Lofty One Who inhabits eternity, whose name is Holy: "I dwell in the high and holy place, With him who has a contrite and **HUMBLE** spirit, To revive the spirit of the **HUMBLE**, And to revive the heart of the contrite ones."

Isaiah 57:15

Holy & Usable for Master's Bountiful Love Everyday

Holy &
Usable for
Master's
Bountiful
Love
Everyday

HOLY EUCHARIST for MASTER'S BOUNTIFUL LOVE EVERYDAY

HUMBLE

Humble Prayer

O God, Your WORD tells me that You require me to walk HUMBLY with You in this journey of life. I ask You, Lord, please teach me to truly HUMBLE myself before You so that You can fulfill Your will through this servant of Yours. Thank You, sweet Jesus, Amen.

*But He gives more **GRACE**.
Therefore He says:
"God resists the proud,
But gives **GRACE**
to the **HUMBLE**."*

James 4:6

GOD'S RIGHTEOUSNESS ALWAYS CASCADING EFFECTIVELY

GRACE

For by **GRACE**
you have been saved
through faith,
and not of yourselves;
it is the gift of God,
not of works,
lest anyone should boast.

Ephesians 2:8-9

GOD'S RIGHTEOUSNESS ALWAYS CASCADING EFFECTIVELY

God's
Righteousness
Always
Cascading
Effectively

And He said to me, "My **GRACE** is sufficient for you, for My strength is made perfect in weakness." Therefore most gladly I will rather boast in my infirmities, that the power of Christ may rest upon me.

2 Corinthians 12:9

GOD'S RIGHTEOUSNESS ALWAYS CASCADING EFFECTIVELY

*Let your speech always be with **GRACE**, seasoned with salt, that you may know how you ought to answer each one.*

Colossians 4:6

Humble Prayer

By Your GRACE, Lord, You have saved such a wretch as I. May I cling to Your righteousness daily, as I walk in Your will and Your way, always showing GRACE to others. I thank You so much for loving me and dying on the cross for me. Thank You for Your unending GRACE.
In sweet Jesus' name I pray, Amen.

Having then

GIFTS

differing according to the

GRACE

that is given to us,
let us use them.

Romans 12:6a

GIFT

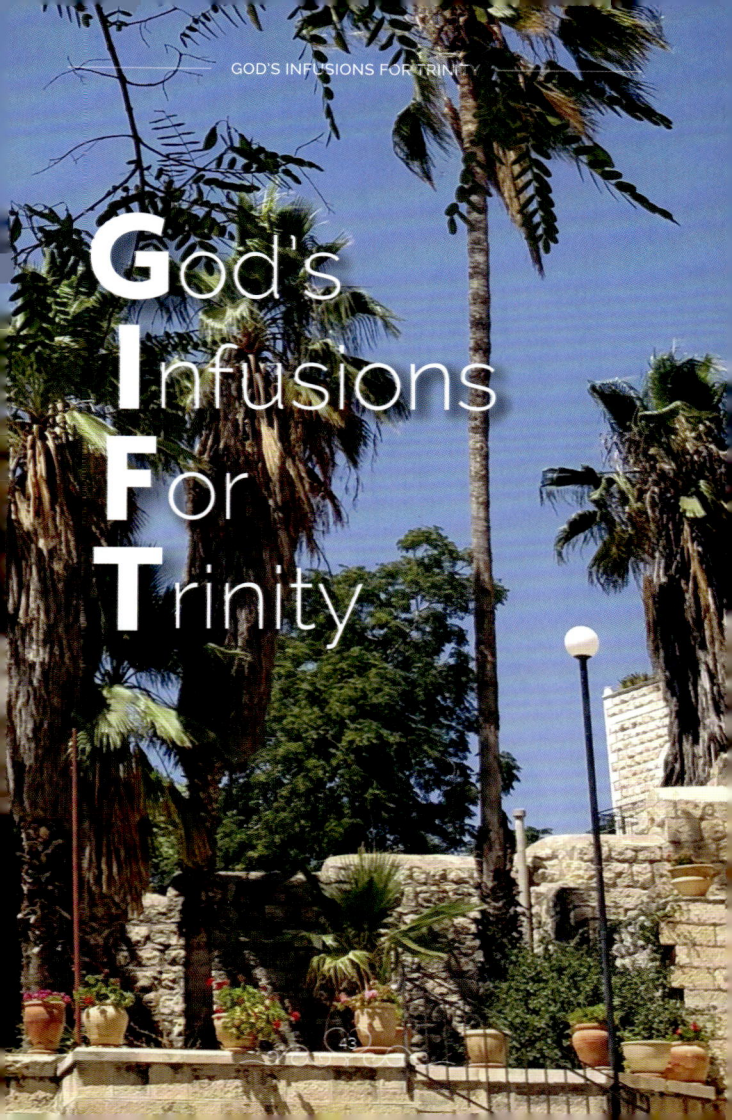

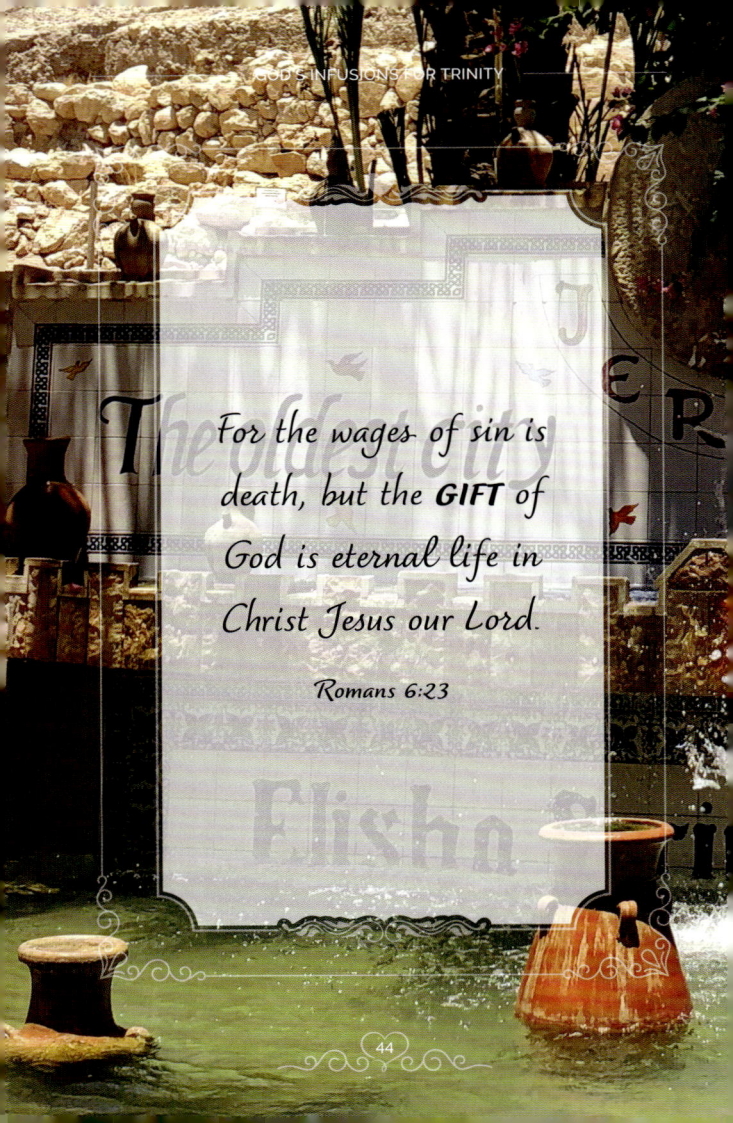

For the wages of sin is death, but the **GIFT** of God is eternal life in Christ Jesus our Lord.

Romans 6:23

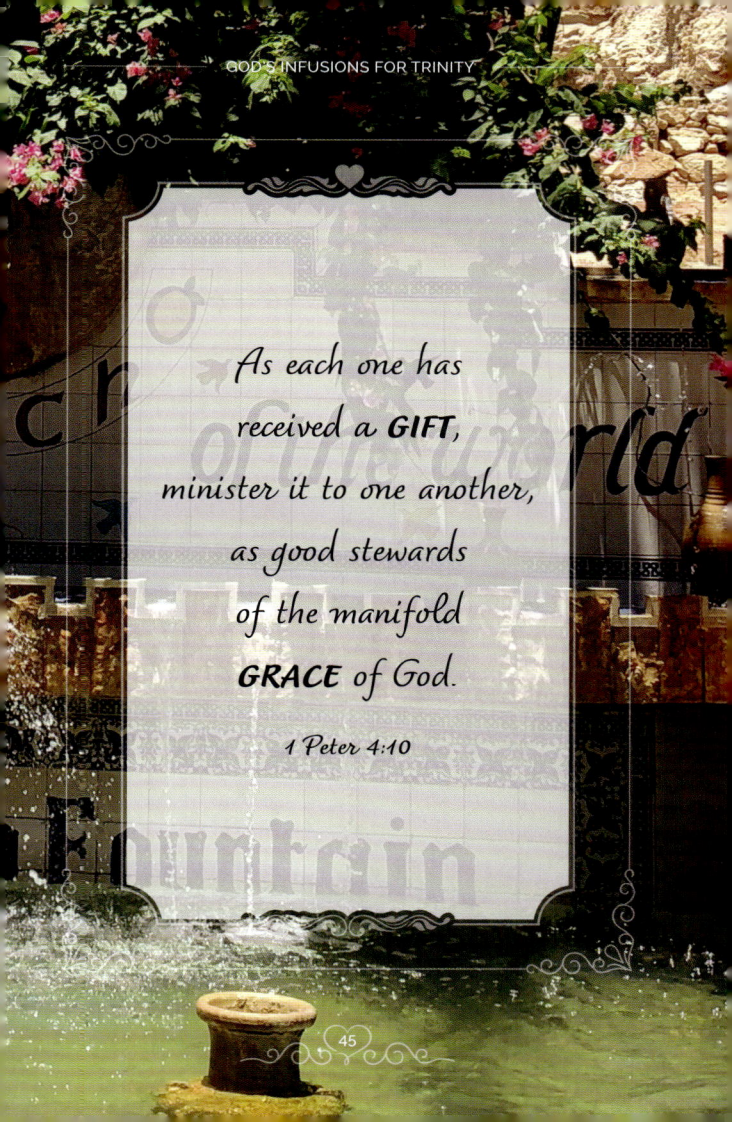

As each one has received a **GIFT**, minister it to one another, as good stewards of the manifold **GRACE** of God.

1 Peter 4:10

GOD'S INFUSIONS FOR TRINITY

GIFT

Humble Prayer

~~~♥~~~

O Heavenly Father, where do I start? You have given me the GIFT of life now and also eternally. You have given me Your most precious GIFT of all, Jesus Christ, Your Son. You have given me the GIFT of Your HOLY SPIRIT indwelling in me. Daily, You continue to bestow unending tangible and spiritual GIFTS upon me. I thank You so much, Lord. May I seek to walk worthy of walking with You and glorify You in everything.

In Jesus' name I pray, Amen.

*Every good **GIFT**
and every perfect **GIFT**
is from above,
and comes down from the
Father of **LIGHTS**, with
whom there is no variation
or shadow of turning.*

James 1:17

LIGHT

Then Jesus spoke to them again, saying, "I am the **LIGHT** of the world. He who follows Me shall not walk in darkness, but have the **LIGHT** of life."

John 8:12

Love
Infused for
Glorifying
Him
Today

LOVE INFUSED for GLORIFYING HIM TODAY

*For with You
is the fountain of life;
In Your **LIGHT**
we see **LIGHT**.*

Psalm 36:9

LOVE INFUSED for GLORIFYING HIM TODAY

"Let your **LIGHT**
so shine before men,
that they may see your
good works
and glorify your Father
in heaven."

Matthew 5:16

LOVE INFUSED for GLORIFYING HIM TODAY

LIGHT

Humble Prayer

Dear Jesus, You are the true LIGHT of the world! May I honor You in being Salt and LIGHT to others as I daily reflect Your glory, while walking in the LIGHT of Your Presence.

In Jesus' name I pray, Amen.

*Blessed are the people who know the **JOYFUL** sound! They walk, O Lord, in the **LIGHT** of Your countenance.*

Psalm 89:15

JOY

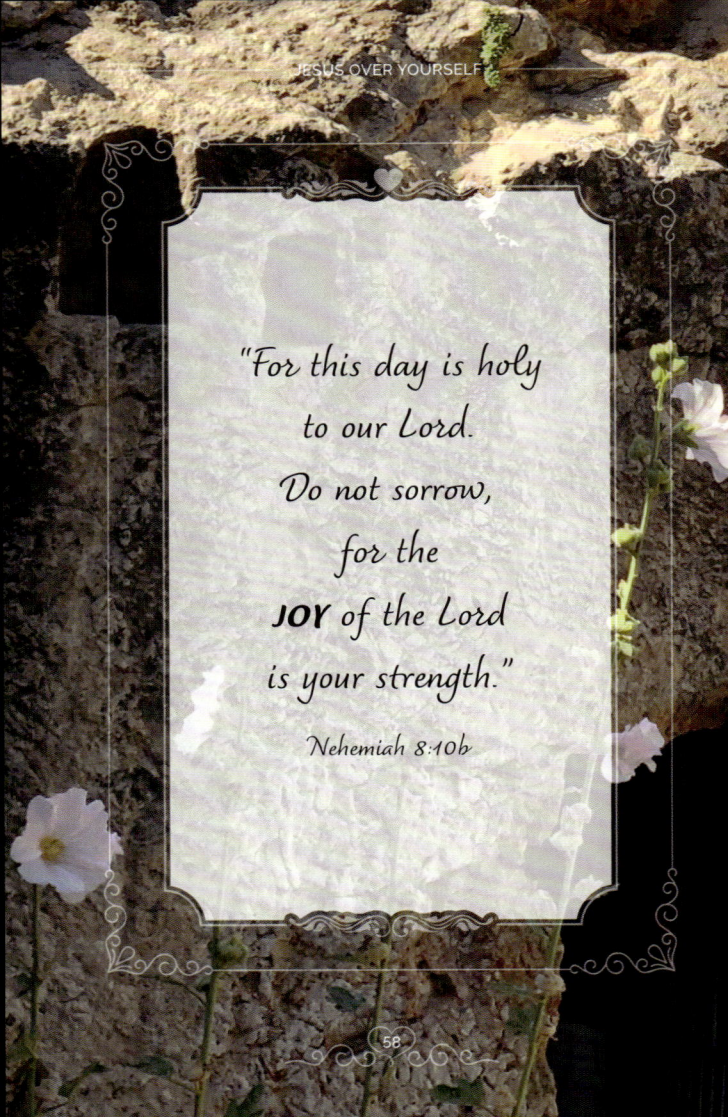

"For this day is holy to our Lord. Do not sorrow, for the **JOY** of the Lord is your strength."

Nehemiah 8:10b

Jesus
Over
Yourself

*Therefore with **JOY**
you will draw water
From the wells
of salvation.*

Isaiah 12:3

> "Until now you have asked nothing in My name. Ask, and you will receive, that your **JOY** may be full."
>
> *John 16:24*

Humble Prayer

O Lord, You are my JOY! As I honor You by walking in the LIGHT and love of Your Presence, may I experience the fullness of Your JOY and always share it with others. Thank You, sweet Jesus, Amen.

"Well done, good and **FAITHFUL** servant; you were **FAITHFUL** over a few things, I will make you ruler over many things. Enter into the **JOY** of your Lord."

Matthew 25:21

FAITH

I have been crucified
with Christ;
it is no longer I who live,
but Christ lives in me;
and the life which
I now live in the flesh
I live by **FAITH**
in the Son of God,
who loved me and
gave Himself for me.

Galatians 2:20

FOLLOW AFTER IMMANUEL TRUSTING HIM

Follow
After
Immanuel
Trusting
Him

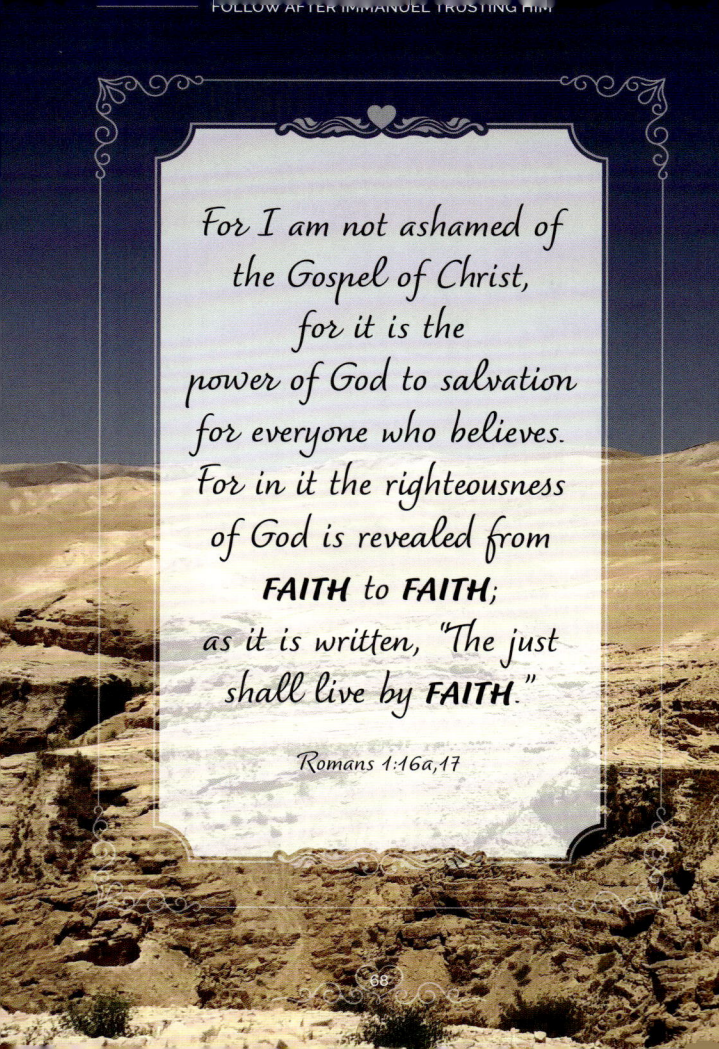

For I am not ashamed of the Gospel of Christ, for it is the power of God to salvation for everyone who believes. For in it the righteousness of God is revealed from **FAITH** to **FAITH**; as it is written, "The just shall live by **FAITH**."

Romans 1:16a,17

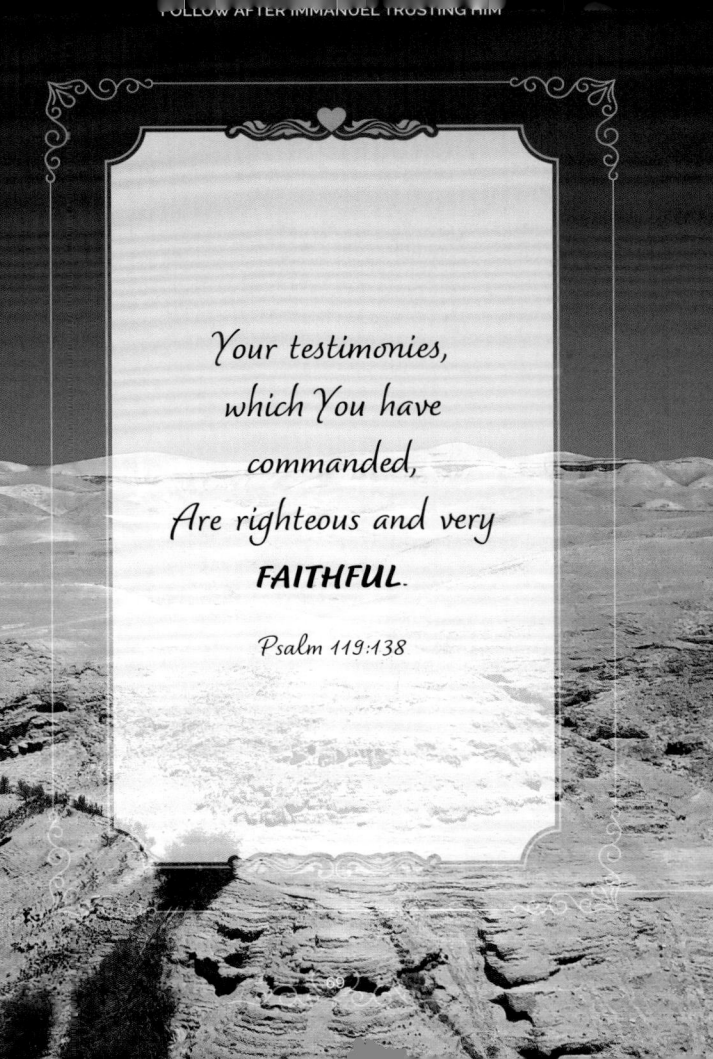

FOLLOW AFTER IMMANUEL TRUSTING HIM

FAITH

FOLLOW AFTER IMMANUEL TRUSTING HIM

Humble Prayer

Dear Heavenly Father, through FAITH in Your Son, I abide in Your WORD and I am Your disciple, therefore;
I am free, yes, free indeed!
Thank You, sweet Jesus, Amen.

*Who through Him believe in God, who raised Him from the dead and gave Him glory, so that your **FAITH** and **HOPE** are in God.*

1 Peter 1:21

HOPE

This **HOPE** we have
as an anchor of the soul,
both sure and steadfast,
and which enters
the Presence
behind the veil.

Hebrews 6:19

Holding **O**nto the **P**resence of **E**mmanuel

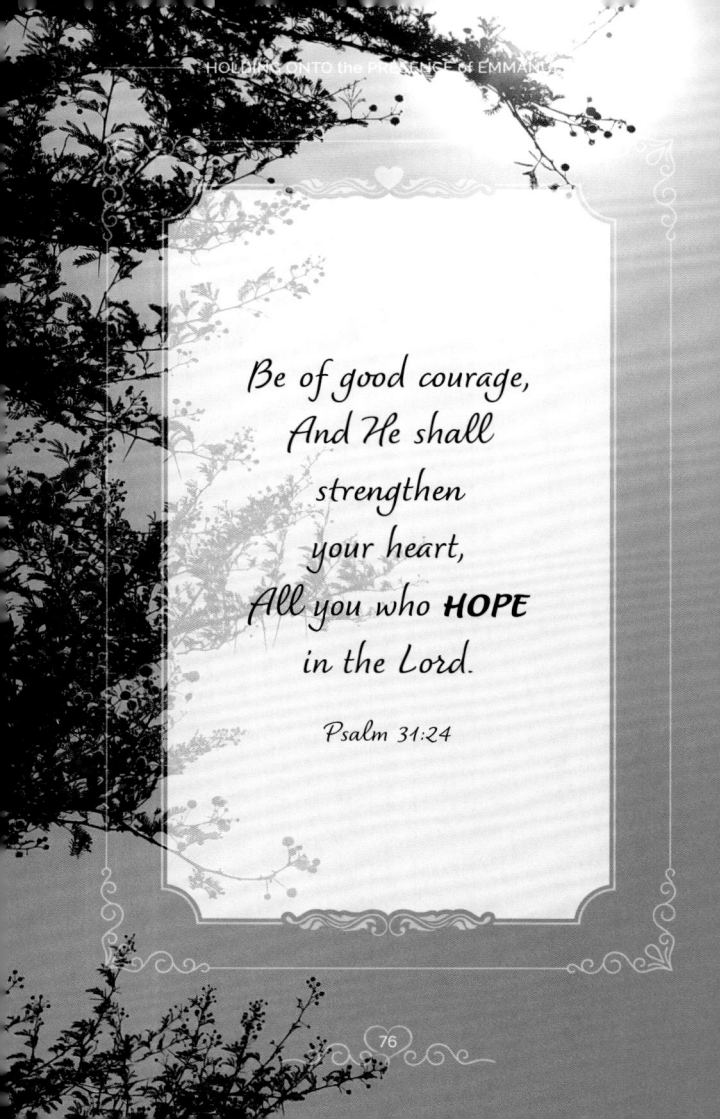

Be of good courage,
And He shall
strengthen
your heart,
All you who **HOPE**
in the Lord.

Psalm 31:24

HOLDING ONTO the PRESENCE of EMMANUEL

"The Lord
is my portion,"
says my soul,
"Therefore
I **HOPE** in Him!"

Lamentations 3:24

Humble Prayer

O Lord, may You be my hiding place and my shield as I study and HOPE in Your WORD. May I abound in HOPE by the Power of Your HOLY SPIRIT. You alone are secure enough to be my anchor in this abundant journey of life.

Thank you, sweet Jesus, Amen.

*"Blessed is the man who **TRUSTS** in the Lord, And whose **HOPE** is the Lord."*

Jeremiah 17:7

TRULY RELEASE UNDERSTANDING to SAVIOR'S TIMING

TRUST

> **TRUST** in the Lord
> with all your heart,
> And lean not on your own
> understanding;
> In all your ways
> acknowledge Him,
> And He shall
> direct your paths.
>
> Proverbs 3:5-6

Truly
Release
Understanding to
Savior's
Timing

TRULY RELEASE UNDERSTANDING to SAVIOR'S TIMING

Preserve me,
O God,
for in You
I put my **TRUST**.

Psalm 16:1

TRULY RELEASE UNDERSTANDING to SAVIOR'S TIMING

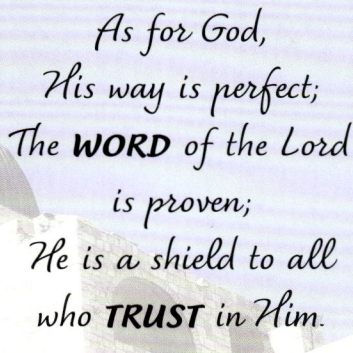

*As for God,
His way is perfect;
The **WORD** of the Lord
is proven;
He is a shield to all
who **TRUST** in Him.*

2 Samuel 22:31
& Psalm 18:30

TRULY RELEASE UNDERSTANDING to SAVIOR'S TIMING

TRUST

Humble Prayer

I TRUST You, Lord. TRUST is the foundation for all relationships. Your way is always best; therefore, I give You control of my life. With simple child-like TRUST, may I always HUMBLY follow where You lead. Thank You for Your guidance in all situations.
In Jesus' name I pray, Amen.

*But let all those rejoice who put their **TRUST** in You; Let them ever shout for **JOY**, because You defend them; Let those also who **LOVE** Your name Be **JOYFUL** in You.*

Psalm 5:11

LIGHT OF VENERATING EMMANUEL

LOVE

LIGHT OF VENERATING EMMANUEL

And now abide
FAITH, HOPE, LOVE,
these three;
but the greatest of these is
LOVE*.*

1 Corinthians 13:13

LIGHT OF VENERATING EMMANUEL

Light
Of
Venerating
Emmanuel

LIGHT OF VENERATING EMMANUEL

LOVE suffers long and is kind; **LOVE** does not envy; **LOVE** does not parade itself, is not puffed up; does not behave rudely, does not seek its own, is not provoked, thinks no evil; does not rejoice in iniquity, but rejoices in the truth; bears all things, believes all things, **HOPES** all things, endures all things. **LOVE** never fails.

1 Corinthians 13:4-8a

Jesus answered him, "The first of all the commandments is: 'Hear, O Israel, the Lord our God, the Lord is One. And you shall **LOVE** the Lord your God with all your heart, with all your soul, with all your mind, and with all your strength.' This is the first commandment. And the second, like it, is this: 'You shall **LOVE** your neighbor as yourself.' There is no other commandment greater than these."

Mark 12:29-31

Closing Humble Prayer

Dear Heavenly Father, thank You so much for LOVING me unconditionally. Thank You for sending Your Son to die on the cross for my sins. I realize that I am a sinner, and I ask You for forgiveness. I surrender my all to You and ask that You please transform me into what You would have me to be. May Your pure and supernatural LOVE shine into my heart, outflowing back to You and to others until I see You face to Face in Heaven. I thank You and I LOVE You, sweet Jesus, Amen.

ACKNOWLEDGEMENTS

A Special heartfelt THANK YOU to:

- Jesus, my Savior…You are my everything!

- My amazing husband, David… for your constant love, support and for guiding our family with God's wisdom.

- My family and friends…for your love and presence in my life.

- Brian Dominey…for your willingness to take on this unique project and making it beautiful with your God-given gift of creativity.

ABOUT THE AUTHOR

Sandra Gladden and "her better half", David, have been married since 1985. They have been enjoying the empty nest since their wonderful son, Will, was married to his precious wife, Rachel, in 2016. Sandra and David make their home in the rural countryside of Fountain Inn, South Carolina and their church home at First Baptist Simpsonville. Together, with the grace of God, over the past 25 years, they have built a successful insurance agency in their neighboring community of Mauldin, where they, and their amazing Team, serve their clients with love. Sandra's passion and favorite pastime activity is studying her Bible. Out of her love for Jesus, she is committed to wholeheartedly enjoying Him, serving Him and following where He leads. God is good!

*The **GRACE** of the Lord Jesus Christ,*
*and the **LOVE** of God,*
*and the communion of the **HOLY SPIRIT***
be with you all. Amen.

2 Corinthians 13:14

My Devotional Thoughts